THE NIAGARA REPORT

Inter-Anglican Publishing Network

Australia

Anglican Information Office
St Andrew's House
Sydney Square
Sydney 2000

Canada

Anglican Book Centre
600 Jarvis Street
Toronto, Ontario M4Y 2J6

Ghana

Anglican Press Ltd
PO Box 8
Accra

India

ISPCK
PO Box 1585
Kashmere Gate
Delhi 11006

Kenya

Uzima Press Ltd
PO Box 48127
Nairobi

New Zealand

Collins Liturgical Publications
PO Box 1
Auckland

Nigeria

CSS Press
50 Broad Street
PO Box 174
Lagos

Southern and Central Africa

Collins Liturgical Publications
Distributed in Southern
Africa by
Lux Verbi, PO Box 1822
Cape Town 8000

Tanzania

Central Tanganyika Press
PO Box 15
Dodoma

Uganda

Centenary Publishing House
PO Box 2776
Kampala

United Kingdom

Church House Publishing
Church House
Great Smith Street
London SW1P 3NZ

United States of America

Forward Movement
 Publications
412 Sycamore Street
Cincinnati, Ohio 45202

THE NIAGARA REPORT

Report of the

Anglican – Lutheran
Consultation on Episcope
Niagara Falls, September 1987

by the Anglican – Lutheran
International Continuation
Committee

PUBLISHED FOR THE
ANGLICAN CONSULTATIVE COUNCIL
AND THE LUTHERAN WORLD FEDERATION

Published 1988 for the Anglican Consultative Council,
Partnership House, 157 Waterloo Road, London, SE1 8UT
and the Lutheran World Federation,
150 Route de Ferney, 1211 Geneva 20, Switzerland.

This edition by
Church House Publishing,
Church House, Great Smith Street
London SW1P 3NZ

ISBN 0 7151 4770 6

Printed by Orphans Press Ltd., Leominster, Herefordshire. Tel. 2460.

Contents

Preface

Two linked events took place at Niagara Falls in autumn 1987 in the course of the international dialogue between Anglicans and Lutherans. The first was a major consultation on *episcope* (24th – 29th September), and this was immediately followed (30th September – 3rd October) by a meeting of the Anglican – Lutheran International Continuation Committee to produce this report.

At the consultation some three dozen theologians, historians and church leaders met to tackle the issue of *episcope,* the chief remaining obstacle to full communion between Anglicans and Lutherans. The intention of this gathering may be summarised thus:

(a) to shed some fresh light on the relationship between the topics of apostolic succession, the ministry of the whole people of God, episcopacy and the historic episcopate;

(b) to set this material in the broad perspective of the Church's mission, taking seriously the diversity of its cultural settings;

(c) and to evaluate in the light of contemporary ecumenical dialogue the current practice of *episcope* amongst Anglicans and Lutherans, so as to offer pointers for the future reform and joint exercise of *episcope* in the service of our common mission.

A wealth of talent and wisdom was contributed to this task, and a real meeting of minds took place on several facets of the subject. There was strong representation from Asia and Africa, where the tempo of Anglican – Lutheran co-operation is visibly quickening. The active participation of Roman Catholic and Eastern Orthodox consultants proved to be very creative. Indeed, the emerging ecumenical consensus reassured Anglicans and Lutherans that their efforts to draw closer to one another in regard to the practical exercise of *episcope* was fully consistent with, and actually assisted by, their current bilateral dialogues with the Roman Catholic Church. Two other factors were specially helpful to the consultation: the daily sharing of worship according to the Anglican and Lutheran traditions, and the peaceful and hospitable atmosphere of Mount Carmel retreat house where we stayed.

Those who took part found this to be a fruitful and stimulating occasion, and it was agreed that the papers contributed should be made available in due course to a wider public by the Anglican Consultative Council (ACC) and the Lutheran World Federation (LWF).

The Anglican – Lutheran Continuation Committee met after the consultation to distil its findings and recommend attainable goals to ACC and LWF. It will be for these parent bodies as well as for individual member churches to decide whether this 'Niagara Report' represents any breakthrough in understanding, and how far and how soon its proposals should be implemented.

We wish to record our warm and grateful thanks to all who contributed to the consultation, and to the secretarial staff, Irmhild Reichen-Young and Vanessa Wilde.

DAVID TUSTIN
Bishop of Grimsby

SEBASTIAN KOLOWA
Presiding Bishop
Evangelical Lutheran Church
in Tanzania

Niagara Falls
October 1987

Abbreviations used in this Report

ACC   Anglican Consultative Council

ALERC   Anglican – Lutheran European Regional Commission

ALIC   Anglican – Lutheran International Conversations

ALICC   Anglican – Lutheran International Continuation Committee

ARCIC   Anglican – Roman Catholic International Commission

BEM   Baptism, Eucharist and Ministry: Faith and Order Paper No. 111

CA   Confessio Augustana: The Augsburg Confession, 1530.

LED II   Lutheran – Episcopal Dialogue Second Series, 1976 – 1980.

LWF   Lutheran World Federation

LRCJC   Lutheran – Roman Catholic Joint Commission

Introduction

1   Official Anglican – Lutheran conversations on the international level extend back over two decades. The first
– the Anglican – Lutheran International Conversations
1970 – 1972 (ALIC) – authorized by the Lambeth Conference and the Lutheran World Federation (LWF) produced the *Pullach Report*.[1] Building upon it, the international relationship was intensified by a planning group
meeting in 1975 and, more especially, by a Joint Working
Group in 1983, which recommended to the Anglican Consultative Council (ACC) and the LWF that they establish
an International Continuation Committee. It should both
enable further international conversation and help to make
the results of the various national and regional Anglican –
Lutheran dialogues contribute to progress elsewhere.

2   At its first meeting in Wimbledon, England, 1986, the
Anglican – Lutheran International Continuation Committee (ALICC) laid plans for a joint consultation on *episcope,*
regarded as the chief obstacle to full communion (see its
report, Appendix III). Its members are listed in Appendix
II. That international consultation took place in Niagara
Falls, Ontario, Canada in September 1987 and provided
the basis for this report. The participants are listed in
Appendix I.

3   Numerous dialogues between Anglicans and Lutherans
during the past twenty years have discovered how much we
share in doctrine, worship, mission, and the understanding

---

[1]For publication details of Reports etc. see Bibliography, p. 68.

and functioning of ministry. The Anglican – Lutheran European Regional Commission (ALERC) concluded that 'there are no longer any serious obstacles on the way towards the establishment of full communion between our two Churches' (*Helsinki Report,* 1982). A further expression of the wide extent of agreement is contained in Section III (paragraphs 60-80) of this present report. But the documents resulting from these official encounters have repeatedly identified differences in the *practice* of *episcope* (that is, pastoral leadership, co-ordination and oversight), especially the presence or absence of bishops in the historic episcopate, as the chief (if not the only remaining) obstacle to full communion. By *historic episcopate* we mean an episcopate which traces its origins back through history to at least the end of the second century. We use the phrase *apostolic succession* in the 'substantive sense' identified by the Lutheran – Roman Catholic Joint Commission (LRCJC) document *The Ministry in the Church* (59,60) to signify 'the apostolicity of the Church in faith' (see further *Baptism, Eucharist and Ministry* (BEM) M 34-5; paragraphs 19, 20 below; *Helsinki Report,* 40 and 43; *Pullach Report,* 1973, 87-89; *LED II,* 1980, pp. 61-62). Thus attention to this topic has been recognized as necessary if we are to

(a) continue movement towards full communion between our respective Churches;

(b) facilitate the ongoing development of common life and mission in various regions where our Churches function in the same geographical areas;

and

(c) open up structural possibilities for the more complete future realization of full communion especially in the countries where our Churches exist side by side.

4   The differences between us in the dimension of *episcope* include not only the presence or absence of bishops in the historic episcopate but also differences in the significance our Churches attach to such bishops. These differences serve as the focal point for mutual fears and suspicions, prejudices and distorted perceptions. They also seem to threaten existing agreements with other Churches as well as ecumenical expectations expressed in dialogues of both our Churches with the Roman Catholic and Orthodox Churches.

5   We have identified, through the work of our predecessors in dialogue and with the assistance of our colleagues in the most recent consultation, some perspectives on this topic which we believe can help our Churches to overcome their differences, as well as ground and shape full communion, and assist its structural expression.

6   In the document which follows, initial and major attention is given to the mission of the Church and its first realization in the communities of the New Testament period (Section I). We give mission such prominence because at Wimbledon 1986 (see Appendix III), our survey of the situation of our Churches throughout the world impressed upon us the fact that the agenda and the timetable for full communion between Anglicans and Lutherans is experienced differently in different parts of the world. However, the urgency of giving attention to the nature of the Church's mission is universal. Indeed, the crisis of the Church in mission is at least as great in those countries in Europe and North America where the need for full communion may be less urgently perceived. At Wimbledon, therefore, we determined that the theme for the consultation on

episcope would be '*Episcope* in Relation to the Mission of the Church'. What we are presenting in Section I

  (i) reflects a significant portion of our work at Niagara,

  (ii) offers a renewed perspective on the mission of the Church as the *gift* of Christ, and

(iii) provides the necessary context for both our understanding of *episcope* and our proposals for the realization of full communion between our Churches.

We conclude that it is a mistake to hold that there is only one criterion which must be satisfied, that of an unbroken chain of ordinations from the apostles' time, if one Church is to recognize another as truly apostolic.

7 Then we seek to identify the major requirements for carrying out the mission of the Church in so far as they concern *episcope* or the ministry of pastoral leadership, co-operation, and oversight (Section II). These are doxology, continuity, disciplined life together, nurture, and faithfulness to the goal of human history given in Jesus Christ. We show how the office of bishop in the early Church sought to hold local churches firm in the *koinonia* or communion of the faithful in all ages (diachronic catholicity) and in all places (synchronic catholicity). We consider subsequent developments in the episcopal office and evaluate Anglican and Lutheran forms of succession in the presiding ministry since the Reformation.

8 The document continues with a summary of 'the truths we share', identifying the common tradition of faith, confession, sacramental life, and perspective on order which Anglicans and Lutherans have discovered in each other (Section III).

9   All this is preparatory to the proposals we make to Anglicans and to Lutherans for the immediate establishment of full communion (Section IV). We conclude this section with a series of proposals for reform which both traditions need to consider in order to renew the ministry of *episcope.*

10   Finally, we identify for our Churches the legislative actions needed, the structures for shared mission and ministry, and the concrete liturgical recognition which would inaugurate our full communion (Section V).

I

The Nature of the Church and its Mission

11   Praise be to the God and Father of our Lord Jesus Christ,
who has bestowed on us in Christ every spiritual blessing
in the heavenly realms. (Eph. 1.3).

The Christian Church is first of all overwhelmingly conscious of the splendour of God's gifts – in Christ we have
been chosen to be dedicated and full of love, to be accepted
as heirs of God, to be forgiven, to be part of a plan that the
whole universe be brought into a unity, and to receive the
seal of the Holy Spirit as a pledge that we shall indeed enter
into that inheritance. But to realize the magnificence of
these gifts the Church continually needs yet another gift,
that of spiritual insight. Only so will we have any concep-
tion of the resources of power open to those who trust in
Christ, resources the scale of which are only measured by
the fact that everything has already been put in subjection
to him, and that this same Christ is the supreme head of the
Church which is his body (Eph. 1.4-23).

12 The life of the Church is based upon this already vic-
torious engagement with the powers of sin and death. It is
the free and unmerited grace of God which, through
Christ's sacrificial death on the cross, once for all, brings us
into union with him. This is how we come to be no longer
aliens, but citizens together with God's own chosen
people. To be the Church is to be part of the story of the
people of God entering into their inheritance within God's
world.

13   But it is precisely that story which reminds us of the difficulties which are to be encountered. The people of Israel, God's chosen people, were repeatedly blind or disobedient, compromised with local rulers, persecuted prophets and suffered horrific disasters. Jesus' own life of teaching, healing and acceptance of the outcast and sinner brought him into deadly rivalry with the prevailing authorities. The disciples whom he sent out were instructed to expect to be rejected as well as received; and the New Testament communities which preserved the stories of Jesus did so in a form which illustrates the fact that jealousy, disputes and misunderstandings were part of their experience even after receiving the gift of the Holy Spirit.

14   There must therefore be a two-fold consciousness in the mind of every Christian; on the one hand of the magnificence of God's gifts, on the other of the need to be prepared for difficulty, struggle and temptation. Honest reading of the history of the Christian Church compels us to admit that that Church, like the people of Israel, has repeatedly been blind or disobedient, has compromised with local rulers, persecuted its prophets and suffered horrific disasters. From that history we learn the necessity for continuous vigilance and the need for penitence.

15   It is the whole Christian Church which has been sent on its mission and been given the necessary gifts. God's plan is the unification of all things in Christ; that, and nothing less, is the goal. Before that goal is realized the Church has the task of embodying in all that it is, says and does the promise that the goal is realizable. The whole Church is witness to that promise, and every member (limb

or organ) of it is inescapably part of how that goal will be understood.

16 In this sense the Church as a whole may be compared to a system of communication, no part of which is strictly irrelevant to the conveying of coherent meaning. When human beings communicate with one another it is important, if one is to avoid confusion, that words, gestures, facial expressions, and symbolic gifts should not contradict each other. Similarly when the Church wishes to be heard in a given culture, it is important that the whole of its 'language' be coherently interrelated so that its message makes sense.

17 Every member of the Church is an integral part of its witness and its mission; and every member has received a gift of the Holy Spirit so that the whole may flourish. 'All members are called to discover, with the help of the community, the gifts they have received and to use them for the building up of the Church and for the service of the world to which the Church is sent' (BEM, M 5. See the whole section, M 1-6, for an expression of the sense that every Christian is involved in the Church's witness to God's plan for humankind.)

18 The outbreak of misunderstandings, personal rivalries and disputes is a threat to the coherence of the Christian mission. It is already clear from the New Testament that the early Christian communities were having to resolve urgent and complex problems specifically relating to their mission and witness. The picture we gain from the study of the New Testament is of communities wrestling with the problems of internal discipline at the same time as carrying

out their mission of witness to the love of God in Jesus Christ.

19 It is in this context that the development of an authoritative, but not authoritarian, ministry must be understood. It is plain that there were from the first those who held specific authority in the churches and who fulfilled their calling in and for the whole community (BEM, M 9). Authority was not a matter of the acquisition of status, but the bestowal of responsibilities. These responsibilities were to be exercised in such a way as to serve the mission of the whole Church in its numerous, diverse, but essentially inter-related acts and attributes. They included the maintenance of 'witness to the apostolic faith, proclamation and fresh interpretation of the Gospel, celebration of baptism and the eucharist, the transmission of ministerial responsibilities, communion in prayer, love, joy and suffering, service to the sick and the needy, unity among the local churches and sharing the gifts which the Lord has given to each' (BEM, M 34).

20 Study of the life of the early Christian communities reflected in the pages of the New Testament should make it unthinkable for us to isolate ordination at the hands of someone in linear succession to the apostles as the sole criterion of faithfulness to the apostolic commission. So many investigations have now confirmed this conclusion that the burden of proof has passed to those who would argue otherwise. Ministries of pastoral leadership, co-ordination and oversight have continuously been part of the Church's witness to the gospel. Indeed we may say that the mission of the Church required the coherence of its witness

in every aspect of its life, and that this coherence required supervision. But the New Testament does not entitle us to assert that such supervision was carried out by a uniform structure of government inherited directly from or transmitted by the apostles (on the development of structures see further paragraphs 41-59). Thus to speak of 'apostolic succession' is to speak primarily of characteristics of the whole Church; and to recognize a Church as being 'in the apostolic succession' is to use not one criterion of discernment, but many (cf. BEM, M 35).

21   It is therefore essential for those Christian Churches which do not enjoy full communion with one another to reappropriate the substantial basis for understanding the apostolic mission of the Church with which the New Testament provides us. Mission indeed comes to special expression in the Church's apostolicity. For apostolicity means that the Church is sent by Jesus to *be* for the world, to participate in his mission and therefore in the mission of the One who sent Jesus, to participate in the mission of the Father and the Son through the dynamic of the Holy Spirit.

22   The Church receives its apostolicity, its mission, as the gift of him who is 'far above all rule and authority and power and dominion, and above every name that is named, not only in this age but also in that which is to come'. For the Father 'has put all things under his feet and has made him the head over all things for the Church, which is his body, the fullness of him who fills all in all' (Eph. 1.21-23). Christ *can* confer his mission upon the Church because by raising him from the dead the Father conferred the final *yes* upon Christ's way of self-offering love. All powers and

dominions in *this* age believe, in the last analysis, that death has the last word. The appropriate expression of such belief is humanity's unrelenting drive for self-preservation. But if the Christ has the last word, then the appropriate expression is rather self-offering, confident in the knowledge that there is more to do with life than preserve it. Those who seek to save their lives will lose them anyway. But those who offer their lives for Christ's sake will find their true selves, will find life itself (Matt. 16.24-26 and parallels).

23   The apostolicity of the Church is the mission of self-offering (not self-preservation) for the life of the world. The Church thus serves the reign of God, not the reign of sin and death. The Church serves the mission of God's suffering and vulnerable love, not a mission of its own devising. The Church serves the mission grounded in and shaped by Christ's way of being in the world.

24   The Kingdom of God is thus the over-arching theme of history. The Church's mission is to witness to that reign by its words and rites (proclamation and sacraments), by its structures and governance (Mark 10.35-45, especially 43), by its *being* as well as its doing. The Church has been given the insight into both the grounding and character of the Kingdom of God (Christ as 'Alpha' and 'way') as well as the final eschatological victory of the Kingdom of God (Christ as 'Omega' and 'fullness' or 'consummation') Because of its *gift* of apostolic mission that Church is called to apostolic mission. In the same way the gift of unity is the basis for the call to be unifying, the gift of holiness is the basis for the call to be consecrating, and the gift of catholicity is the basis for the call to be whole, orthodox and universal.

II

Requirements for the Church's Mission

25   The *gift* of Christ is that he sends his disciples as he has been sent (John 20.21), that they are to witness to God's forgiving judgement and verdict by setting at liberty all who are in the bondage of sin, that they are to witness to God's confounding and defeat of evil by unmasking the demonic powers and joining the struggle against them. In Christ the Church is called to have and to serve the 'keys' of the kingdom of God (Matt. 16.18). In Christ the Church is called to be a sign, an instrument and a foretaste of the kingdom of God.

26   The Church awakens to the astonishing discovery that its mission is a gift, that it has indeed been given the pearl of great price, the treasure hidden in a field (Matt. 13.44-46) and that this discovery is the reason for gathering others in order to participate in the joy (Luke 15.8-10). In order to *be* such a Church it becomes conscious that certain things are required of it. These 'requirements' follow as consequences upon the discovery that its mission is in fact a gift.

Doxology

27   The Church praises God 'for our creation, preservation, and all the blessings of this life; but above all for (God's) inestimable love in the redemption of the world by our Lord Jesus Christ; for the means of grace, and for the

hope of glory' (Book of Common Prayer, General Thanksgiving). It has been given the word of Christ for teaching, admonition, wisdom as it sings and preaches, in prison and out of it (Acts 16.25), 'with thankfulness ... to God' (Col. 3.16). It is called 'in word or deed (to) do everything in the name of the Lord Jesus, giving thanks to God the Father through him' (Col. 3.17). It has been baptized a royal priesthood as a people claimed by God for his own to proclaim the triumphs of one who has called us out of darkness into his marvellous light (1 Pet. 2.9). It has been given the meal by which it receives with thanksgiving the final, full and costly sacrifice of Christ on the cross. In this meal the Church has been given its identity as the community which anticipates the heavenly banquet of consummated salvation (Isa. 25.6-8; Matt. 26.29; Mark 14.25; Luke 22.16, 18; Matt. 14.19 and parallels; Luke 13.29; Luke 14.15-24; John 6.30-59; Rev. 19.9). In this meal the Church has been given the promise that in Christ God will receive the offering of the whole people whom God calls and uses in the apostolic mission of the Kingdom (Rom. 12.1-21). In the doxological prayer of the Kingdom the Son gives the Church the Father's name as the One who sent him in the power of the Spirit (Luke 11.1-13). The Church praises the Triune Name and prays in that name in order to be grasped and shaped by it for participation in the divine mission.

Continuity

28   The God who calls the Church to its divine mission is faithful. God is faithful to God's own being and identity. The act of calling the universe into being is an act of

vulnerable, risk-taking love (John 1.9-18; Col. 1.15-20; Heb. 13.8). God is faithful in covenant and promise, not abandoning Israel, but giving up the Son 'for us all' (Rom. 8.31-39) so that the Gentiles might be grafted on to the 'olive tree' of the people of God (Rom. 11.1-32). It is God's *faithfulness* which is 'unsearchable' and 'inscrutable' and which evokes our praise (Rom. 11.33-36). The Church is given the gift of God's fidelity in order to be faithful. It has God's continuity in order to continue in Christ's word and to abide in *koinonia* or communion with Christ and with each other – and thus to experience and express both truth and freedom (John 8.31-33). The context in which the continuity of ministerial office is presented in the Pastoral Epistles is faithful teaching and confession (1 Tim. 4.6-16; 6.3-16; 2 Tim. 2.1-6; Titus 2.1).

29   Because the Church's call to faithfulness and continuity is grounded in God's faithfulness and continuity, it is possible for the Church to cherish both those symbols of continuity which the Church has been given and also those experiences in its past in which God's faithfulness has persevered despite the Church's brokenness, ambiguity, perversity and unfaithfulness. The Church acknowledges with thanksgiving the canonical Scriptures through which Torah and prophets, apostolic proclamation and gospel narrative have been identified, gathered and transmitted. The Church exists because of the unbroken continuity of the gift of baptism and the Lord's Supper. The Church has been given the gift of orthodox confession in the form of dogmatic response to heresies which threatened the gospel. The Church receives gratefully whatever historical continuity its bishops and presbyters have been given.

30   Such symbols of continuity are, however, only part of the life of the Church, and need constantly to be interpreted afresh so that their meaning and impact may be always experienced as the liberating gospel of God's grace. Like any living being, the Church only remains what it is through change and adjustment. The mere preservation of symbols of continuity may diminish their effectiveness. The history of the Christian Church contains the record of God's faithfulness in spite of human faithlessness. God has persevered with the Church even when the Scriptures have been mutilated, ignored, traduced or idolized; even when baptism has been administered promiscuously or received frivolously; even when the Lord's Supper has become routine or been neglected; even when the loss of the connection between gospel and dogma has led to inquisition and authoritarianism on the one hand, rejection and apostasy on the other hand. In the context of our study of *episcope* we have been led to trust God's faithfulness also when bishops in historic succession have been unfaithful in an effluvium of evil, or when churches forced to endure ruptures in the tradition grew comfortable with their supposed autonomy. The gospel of God's faithfulness is at the same time his call to the Church to repent and be reconciled.

Disciplined Life Together as a Community of Disciples

31   The Church's mission is given by God to a community. This has its basis in both the mission and the obedience of Jesus. The mission of Jesus was directed to Israel as a people, to Israel's renewal of and recalling of *its* mission (Luke 2.29-32; Matt. 10.5-15 and parallels; Matt. 15.24).

Through the renewal of Israel and the calling of the twelve the eschatological vision of the gathering of the Gentiles and the overcoming of alienation was to be realized (Eph. 2.11 – 3.13). The separate existence of synagogue (which does not acknowledge Jesus as Messiah) and Church (which confesses Jesus as Messiah) is a painful reminder that our sinfulness continues to frustrate the mission of God, that we live in the tension between the inauguration and consummation of the Kingdom of God, that the Church itself is an ambiguous and incomplete sign of the Kingdom of God. The temptation to autonomous individualism and anarchy on the one hand and to oppressive collectivism on the other hand means that the Church requires discipline in its corporate life and at the same time that such discipline needs to be grounded in the obedience of Christ. The Church is a community of disciples (Matt. 28.19-20). Its discipleship is described by the 'Torah' of the Kingdom of God (e.g. Matt. 5-7) and the apostolic description of life in the disciple community (e.g. Rom. 12 – 15; Gal. 5 – 6, Col. 2.20 – 4.6; Eph. 4 – 6). The discipline is both grounded in and shaped by Christ. Leadership is not to be like that of the Gentiles (Mark 10.43). It is 'in the Lord' (1 Thess. 5.12-13; Eph. 5.21). It begins with the mind of Christ who took the form of a servant and was obedient to a slave's death (Phil. 2.1-11). Yet it is discipline replete with admonition (Mark and Matthew are written to communities to correct them and their leadership, as are Galatians, both Corinthian letters, 1 Thessalonians, and more) and making painful decisions necessary (e.g. 1 Cor. 5.1-2). The freedom of the gospel is the freedom of all in the community to be committed to the holiness of one another and the wholeness of the community (Gal. 6.1-5). Love is never indifferent.

Nurture

32   Here again the Church discovers that the resource for its mission has already been given it. For Christ himself is the living bread, given for the life of the world (John 6.51). He is the living water, of which, if anyone drinks, that person will never thirst again (John 4.14). Christ is, moreover, the door of the sheepfold, through which the sheep will pass to find somewhere safe to graze (John 10.9). These images of nurture become the task of the Church by virtue of the commission to Peter to feed Christ's lambs (John 21.15). Nurture lies at the root of the exhortation for tenderness towards the 'little ones', by which may be meant not just children but the young in the faith. Whether such persons may be fed milk or are ready for meat calls for the exercise of discernment (1 Cor. 3.2; Heb. 3.12).

33   The apparently reassuring imagery of shepherding conceals sharp judgements and urgent demands. The reason why sheep become the prey of wild beasts is because of bad shepherds who consume the milk, wear the wool, slaughter the fat beasts or drive them with ruthless severity (Ezek. 34.1-10). This indeed is the reason why the Lord himself is the shepherd of his people who, unlike the hireling, is ready to give his life for the sheep. Human shepherds of God's flock need to be reminded of his example and to guard against the temptations of power, if they are to receive the approval of the Chief Shepherd at his appearance (1 Pet. 5.1-4).

34   The life of the Church can draw not merely upon Christ as a resource, but also must look toward Christ as

the goal of its growth. Its maturity will be measured by nothing less than the full stature of Christ (Eph. 4.13). Nor is this conceived of as individual growth; it is, rather, the 'building up of the body of Christ', in which there is a variety of gifts each designed 'to equip God's people for work in God's service' (Eph. 4.12). There is, of course, a possibility, of which St Paul himself clearly has examples in mind, that such gifts might be deployed competitively: the eye and the hand in fact need each other and may have to be told so (1 Cor. 12.14-26). Even the simple acts of planting and watering the seed of the Word need to be seen as co-operative ('they work as a team', 1 Cor. 3.8 NEB). The mission of the Church requires a continuous effort to con-ceive all the Holy Spirit's gifts as part of a single enterprise and the overcoming of the tendency of human beings to jealousy and overbearing behaviour. The task of nurture is thus inseparable from that disposition of mind which is ready to reckon others better than oneself (Phil. 2.3).

Direction and Goal

35   The journey on which the Church is engaged has a goal and a direction which shape the whole character of the mission of the people of God from the beginning. In the ministry, death and resurrection of Jesus the Church has been given a vision of the outcome of history. All things are to be brought into a unity in Christ (Eph. 1.10). It is, therefore, to Jesus Christ that we look while running with resolution the race for which we are entered (Heb. 12.1-2). In him we have the confidence to view the future as the triumph of the Kingdom of God (Rev. 5; Rev. 7.13-17: cf. Isa. 25.6-8). We are the people who know the final out-

come of the story, without yet knowing the details of the plot. Indeed, because the Church has been let in on the outcome of the story of the world, the Church's life and witness *change* the plot of history.

36 Because the outcome of history has been disclosed in Jesus, the Church is called to anticipate the future of the Messianic age by sharing the Messianic banquet (see 27 above), the Lord's Supper. But when the Church does not include 'those who have nothing', when it does not care about the world's poor, then it no longer partakes of the *Lord's* Supper. The Church not only profanes 'the body and blood of the Lord', it also denies its own identity as the people of the new age, the Messianic age (1 Cor. 11.17-34).

37 Because the outcome of history has been disclosed in Jesus, the Church receives a *living hope* through the resurrection of Jesus Christ from the dead (1 Pet. 1.3-9). In Jesus' death and resurrection the power of death to determine the future has been broken. Death cannot have the last word for those who believe the resurrection. We now live toward the future differently, as a self-offering, not a self-protective, people. Our future is shaped by the one who has death behind him. He has become the 'first fruits' of those who sleep (1 Cor. 15.20-28). Hence the Church is free to offer itself even to death, its ultimate witness (*martyria*) to its hope. The Church is thus free to relate to enemies in a radically new way (1 Pet. 2.20-25; 3.9-12; Matt. 5.38-48; Luke 6.29-30; Rom. 12.17). The Church witnesses to the Messianic age by its commitment to peace (Micah 3.3-4; Isa. 2.2-4).

38 Because the outcome of history has been disclosed in Jesus, the Church is committed to justice for victims, and to liberation for the oppressed (Luke 1.51-53; 4.16-21; Matt. 11.5). The Church seeks to express in its own life the overcoming of every alienation, whether racist, sexist, or economic (Gal. 3.27-28).

39 Because the outcome of history has been disclosed in Jesus, the Church is set free to view the past differently. The earliest disciples now could understand the cross of Jesus not as the rejection of his messianic mission but as the way of the Messiah. (Luke 24.26 is but one example. Isaiah 53 came to be understood as messianic only after the resurrection of Jesus.) Indeed, the cross of Christ is God's true glory (John 12.27-36; 17.1-15). Moreover, the disciples are called to the way of the cross, to suffer for the sake of the gospel (Mark 8.34-35 and parallels, Heb. 13.12-13). The disciples are also free to discern their *own* past differently, to confess sin rather than to deceive themselves by denying sin, to trust God's justification rather than their own self-contrived justifications.

40 Because of the vision which shapes its future the Church recognizes that its mission is both necessary and limited; that the Kingdom of God is served beyond the Church; and that God may often have to work despite and against the Church. Because the Church betrays its mission it requires *episcope* to recall it, rebuke it and reform it.

Development of Structure

41 All these requirements for the mission of the Church in time are given in Christ, yet need to be realized in

history. Each one – the praise of the community, its faithfulness and continuity, its disciplined life together, its activity of nurture and its sense of goal and direction – must be focused in symbolic acts and structures. As the Church was launched outwards into the cultures of the ancient world and encountered new problems and dangers for which it had no ready-made solutions, these were the hallmarks of its common life.

42 As we have already remarked, there is no single pattern of leadership common to the early Christian communities (see paragraphs 19-20 above). Nevertheless, there was a serious and persisting need for wise and faithful leadership in the mission of the Church. 'Ministerial office played an essential part in the life of the Church in the first century ... Normative principles governing the purpose and function of the ministry are already present in the New Testament documents (e.g. Mark 10.43-45; Acts 20.28; 1 Tim. 4.12-16; 1 Pet. 5.1-4). The early churches may well have had considerable diversity in the structure of pastoral ministry, though it is clear that some churches were headed by ministers who were called *episcopoi* and *presbyteroi*. While the first missionary churches were not a loose aggregation of autonomous communities, we have no evidence that 'bishops' and 'presbyters' were appointed everywhere in the primitive period. The terms 'bishop' and 'presbyter' could be applied to the same man or to men with identical or very similar functions' (Anglican – Roman Catholic International Commission (ARCIC), *The Final Report,* Ministry and Ordination 6).

43 The deaths of St Paul, St Peter and St James (the Lord's brother), who had exercised authoritative ministries

in the churches, though in different places and in differing ways, left a vacuum in the Church's life. The Book of Acts reflects the steps which were taken to supply this lack, by the appointment of presbyters (Acts 14.23). But the New Testament exhibits a striking absence of interest in titles or official designations when we compare the Christian writings with material concerning voluntary associations in the ancient world. The gospels of St Matthew and of St John show awareness of the danger inherent in the developing structures and offices. 1 Peter warns against authoritarianism and money-making in the church leadership of northern Asia Minor. Though there is great interest in the Pastoral Epistles in the means for ensuring the succession of leadership by the laying on of hands, there is no evidence to suggest that the bishop or presbyter had an exclusive role in relation to baptism and the eucharist.

44 There is a limited amount of testimony about the structures of Christian community in the second century. All fourth-century and later testimony about this period must be handled with care because ancient writings about church history placed primary importance on proving there had been a consistent, unchanging Christian tradition. (In this, ancient Christian authors accepted the general cultural preference for what was old: the new was suspect on principle.) By the fourth century, the 'monarchical episcopate' was so standard and unquestioned that it came to be regarded as having apostolic origins.

45 Ignatius of Antioch (*c.* 117) provides us with the earliest mention of the threefold ministry. But the episcopate he describes is what might be called a congregational episcopate as opposed to the later regional episcopate.

Ignatius saw the bishops as standing in God's place, presiding over the community. The presbyters were seen either as 'God's Council' or the 'Council of Apostles' – thus evoking the scene of the last judgement. The deacons represented either the commandment of God or Jesus Christ. In any case, 'we are not certain how the Ignatian bishop was appointed or that he stood in a chain of historic succession to the apostles by means of ordination or even that the pattern described by Ignatius was universal in the church' (Lutherans and Catholics in Dialogue IV, *Eucharist and Ministry,* 39. Reflections of the Roman Catholic participants).

46   Churches increasingly found that political or quasi-political terminology expressed their sense of their own identity. This language was already to be found in the New Testament. Christians were a new people, or a new race, whose *politeuma* or commonwealth was in heaven (Phil. 3.20), strangers and sojourners in other people's cities in one sense, but looking forward to the city which God had prepared for them (Heb. 11.16) and thus in another sense at home in God's world. In their local communities, therefore, Christian people came to see themselves less and less as a specialized organization and more and more as a kind of tight-knit *polis* within a *polis,* whose interests and activities embraced not some, but all, of the normal concerns of their members. The Church spread throughout the Roman world was one body, a single 'people'; and it was of such a body that the bishop came to be recognized as leader and principal officer in each locality.

47   As time went on, the churches responded to the variety of gifts present in their midst by the creation of

numerous other roles – readers, catechists, exorcists, acolytes, virgins and the like – all of whom were called *clerici*, in distinction to the ordinary citizenry, or *laici*. These developments indicate the openness of the churches to a variety of forms of ministry, not all of which needed to be perpetuated. But all alike, 'clergy' and 'laity', were first and foremost citizens of the commonwealth of heaven, all alike members of God's household (Eph. 2.19). When that household met together the bishop presided in a way which marked him out as the symbolic person in whom the identity of the community was focused and represented.

48   The significance of these developments is not that they can be extracted from the seamless web of church history and given normative status. Their importance lies rather in the basic intention to which they gave expression. The churches, in becoming discrete cultures within cultures, constituted a system of symbols. The office of bishop was valued because it expressed something important to the Church's self-identity both within the community and in its external relations. It was a development relevant to a particular time and place, but with some surprising features – for example that bishops, unlike local magistrates, were elected for life. All our evidence confirms that, whatever the theological understanding of the office, it was open to gross abuse, as the New Testament documents already had made clear of earlier patterns of leadership.

49   But it had two clear advantages: first, that because the whole people was involved in the election (perhaps by shouting their votes – the potential for riotous disorder was always present), the authority of the bishop lay, in

part, in the recognition accorded him by the community in its entirety; and secondly, ordinations entailed the participation of bishops from neighbouring congregations and thus elicited at least their consent. In the course of time, the role which neighbouring bishops played in the process of selection increased in importance, as stress was laid on the unity of the world-wide Church. Thus the bishop embodied in his office the tension between locality and universality. In virtue of his election he represented the Christian people of his own town for the universal Church; and in virtue of the assent of the larger Church, symbolized by the mode of his ordination, he represented for his own flock the universal people of God, the whole body of local churches knit together in the communion of Christ.

50 The handling of this tension was no easy matter. Bishops installed by outside authority sometimes had great difficulty in governing their local churches; and bishops who were popular with their own flocks were sometimes judged unsatisfactory by synods of their peers. In the course of time more and more of the initiative for the election of bishops came to rest in the hands of regional authorities until the development reached the point that no bishop could be installed without the consent of the metropolitan.

51 By the fourth century also a significant realignment of responsibilities was occurring within the threefold ministry. The bishop, who had been in principle the leader of a single congregation, had become a regional overseer, while the presbyters, who had had no independent liturgical function, became the presidents of local eucharistic assemblies. By the Middle Ages this shift led to the presbyter's ministry being taken for the normative form of

ministry. The difference between bishop and presbyter was now a matter of jurisdiction. Jerome's opinion that bishops and presbyters were originally one and the same became widely accepted and played a role in both the Lutheran and Anglican Reformations.

52   Once again it must be said that this history is not invoked in order to give it normative status. There is too much variety for us to construct a single, synthetic picture of the episcopal office; and there is always a danger in anachronistically reading back the vastly changed scale of a modern bishop's activities into the ancient communities which were smaller. The point is rather that the symbolic position occupied by the bishop had two dimensions, the spatial and the temporal. The connections between the local and the universal, the present and the past, are both aspects of the one *koinonia* or communion. On the one hand, the bishop 'is responsible for preserving and promoting the integrity of the *koinonia* in order to further the Church's response to the Lordship of Christ and its commitment to mission' (ARCIC, *The Final Report,* Authority I, 5); a *koinonia* which 'is realized not only in the local Christian communities, but also in the communion of these communities with one another' (ibid., 8). On the other hand the bishop as confessor of the faith links the church with its foundation in the prophetic and apostolic scriptures (Eph. 2.20).

53   What is essential to the life and mission of the Church is that the connection between the universal and the local should be made, and that it should be effective. The question which has to be addressed to our own churches is not merely whether they intend such a link, but how it is

allowed to be effective. The mere presence of a bishop as what is said to be 'a focus of unity' will not *guarantee* the preservation of *koinonia* between local and universal; nor will the absence of such a bishop entail its destruction. The case is the same in relation to continuity. 'Apostolic succession in the episcopal office does not consist primarily in an unbroken chain of those ordaining to those ordained, but in a succession in the presiding ministry of a church which stands in the continuity of apostolic faith and which is overseen by the bishop in order to keep it in the communion of the Catholic and Apostolic Church' (LRCJC, *The Ministry in the Church,* 62).

54 Our brief reference to episodes in the history of the episcopal office highlights a telling fact. It is the oversight or presiding ministry which constitutes the heart of the episcopal office, and that oversight is never to be viewed apart from the continuity of apostolic faith. The fact of bishops does not by itself guarantee the continuity of apostolic faith. A material rupture in the succession of presiding ministers does not by itself guarantee a loss of continuity in apostolic faith. What evaluation is, then, to be given of a situation in which there is a material rupture in the succession of presiding ministers in the name of preserving the continuity of apostolic faith?

55 Clearly, no simple answer can be given. Where the rupture occurs, subsequent steps taken to secure the continuity of apostolic faith and to provide for a new succession in presiding ministry must weigh heavily in making that evaluation. In the English Reformation, it may be argued, the episcopal succession was secured in an

uncanonical fashion in that no currently sitting diocesan bishops could be found who were willing to consecrate Matthew Parker. Whatever may be said about this and about the sufficiency of the 1550 Ordinal for the transmission of the historic threefold ministry, the Preface to the Ordinal witnessed to the intention of the English Reformers to continue that ministry in a reformed manner. Thus the importance of the Ordinal does not lie in the historical accuracy of its claim that the offices of bishop, presbyter and deacon were present in the Church from the beginning. Its importance lies rather in its expression of the intention to preserve continuity with traditional church structures.

56   For the Lutheran Reformation too the situation was complicated by the refusal of sitting bishops to ordain pastors for evangelical congregations. Faced with this emergency, 'the Wittenberg Reformation sought a new understanding of ordained ministry by reaching back to the ordering of the Ancient Church. In so doing, the ministry of oversight in the (Wittenberg) *Stadtkirche* was described as an episcopal office and services of ordination were broadly structured to be a reappropriation of episcopal consecration in the Ancient Church' (*Kirchengemeinschaft in Wort und Sakrament,* Hannover 1984, p. 75). The Reformers 'ordained through ordained pastors and thus laid claim to the episcopal structure of the office of pastors (ministers).' (H. Fries and K. Rahner, *Unity of the Churches,* Philadelphia 1985, p. 94).

57   It must be clearly noted that the Reformers believed themselves authorized to act in this manner in an emergency situation, appealing to Jerome's position on the

original unity of the office of bishop and presbyter. The authority of a bishop's office is thus present in the pastors. The succession of a presiding ministry is thus preserved, though in an unaccustomed form. There was no objection to the office of bishop as such, as the Augsburg Confession testifies:

> St Peter forbids the bishops to exercise lordship as if they had power to coerce the churches according to their will. It is not our intention to find ways of reducing the bishops' power, but we desire and pray that they may not coerce our consciences to sin. If they are unwilling to do this and ignore our petition, let them consider how they will answer for it in God's sight, inasmuch as by their obstinacy they offer occasion for division and schism, which they should in truth help to prevent (CA, XVIII, 76-78).

58 A similar problem faces both Anglicans and Lutherans, namely that the succession in the presiding ministry of their respective churches no longer incontestably links those churches to the *koinonia* of the wider Church.

59 The comprehensive doctrinal agreement between Lutherans and Anglicans outlined in Section III indicates a commonly held apostolic faith. In the light of this commonly held apostolic faith, neither tradition can, in good conscience, reject the apostolic nature of the other. In the light of the argument contained in the above sections, the ordained ministry is no longer an issue which need divide our two Churches. In the light of the symbolic position of the bishop as reflecting both the universal and local *koinonia,* the continued isolation, one from another, of those who exercise this office of *episcope* in our two Churches is no longer tolerable and must be overcome.

III

The Truths We Share

60   The Anglican – Lutheran European Regional Commission *Helsinki Report,* of 1982, observed that 'the history of Anglican – Lutheran relations is a complex one and cannot be reduced to one simple pattern' (paragraph 13). It is not necessary for us to trace all of the reasons for this observation. One fact, however, stands out. These two traditions have not officially engaged in any divisive theological or doctrinal controversies. They have not officially condemned each other as Churches. Conversations in recent years in Europe, North America, and Australia have resulted in identifying large areas of agreement in faith and life. Shared work and witness in Africa and Asia have revealed similar areas of agreement. In the USA, most Lutherans and the Episcopal Church have entered into formal agreement of 'interim Eucharistic Sharing' with each other. We wish here to specify the truths we share as disclosed by our official conversations.[1]

61   We accept the authority of the canonical Scriptures of the Old and New Testaments. We read the Scriptures liturgically in the course of the Church's year *(Lutheran - Episcopal Dialogue II* (LED II), 1980, pp. 30-1; *Pullach Report,* 17-22).

---

[1] The most convenient collection of the relevant documents is to be found in *What Can We Share?* A Lutheran – Episcopal Resource and Study. William A. Norgren, editor. Cincinnati, Forward Movement Publications, 1985. Also *Growth in Agreement,* Reports and Agreed Statements of Ecumenical Conversations on a World Level, Harding Meyer and Lukas Vischer, editors, New York and Geneva, Paulist Press and WCC, 1984.

62 We accept the Niceno – Constantinopolitan and Apostles' Creeds and confess the basic Trinitarian and Christological Dogmas to which these creeds testify. That is, we believe that Jesus of Nazareth is true God and true Man, and that God is authentically identified as Father, Son and Holy Spirit (LED II, p. 38; *Pullach Report,* 23-25).

63 Anglicans and Lutherans use very similar orders of service for the Eucharist, for the Prayer Offices, for the administration of Baptism, for the rites of Marriage, Burial, and Confession and Absolution. We acknowledge in the liturgy both a celebration of salvation through Christ and a significant factor in forming the *consensus fidelium.* We have many hymns, canticles, and collects in common (*Helsinki Report,* 29-31).

64 We believe that baptism with water in the name of the Triune God unites the one baptized with the death and resurrection of Jesus Christ, initiates into the One, Holy, Catholic and Apostolic Church, and confers the gracious gift of new life (*Helsinki Report,* 22-25).

65 We believe that the Body and Blood of Christ are truly present, distributed and received under the forms of bread and wine in the Lord's Supper. We also believe that the grace of divine forgiveness offered in the sacrament is received with the thankful offering of ourselves for God's service (LED II, pp. 25-29; *Helsinki Report,* 26-28).

66 We believe and proclaim the gospel, that in Jesus Christ God loves and redeems the world. We 'share a common understanding of God's justifying grace, i.e. that

we are accounted righteous and are made righteous before God only by grace through faith because of the merits of our Lord and Saviour Jesus Christ, and not on account of our works or merit. Both our traditions affirm that justification leads and must lead to ''good works''; authentic faith issues in love' *(Helsinki Report,* 20; cf. LED II, pp. 22-23).

67   Anglicans and Lutherans believe that the Church is not the creation of individual believers, but that it is constituted and sustained by the Triune God through God's saving action in word and sacraments. We believe that the Church is sent into the world as sign, instrument and foretaste of the kingdom of God. But we also recognize that the Church stands in constant need of reform and renewal *(Helsinki Report,* 44-51).

68   We believe that all members of the Church are called to participate in its apostolic mission. They are therefore given various ministries by the Holy Spirit. Within the community of the Church the ordained ministry exists to serve the ministry of the whole people of God. We hold the ordained ministry of word and sacrament to be a gift of God to his Church and therefore an office of divine institution *(Helsinki Report,* 32-42).

69   We believe that a ministry of pastoral oversight *(episcope)*, exercised in personal, collegial and communal ways, is necessary to witness to and safeguard the unity and apostolicity of the Church *(Pullach Report,* 79).

70   We share a common hope in the final consummation of the kingdom of God and believe that we are compelled to work for the establishment of justice and peace. The obligations of the Kingdom are to govern our life in the Church and our concern for the world. 'The Christian faith is that God has made peace through Jesus "by the blood of his Cross" (Col. 1.20) so establishing the one valid centre for the unity of the whole human family' (Anglican – Reformed International Commission 1984: *God's Reign and Our Unity,* 18 and 43; cf. *Pullach Report,* 59).

71   Because of all that we share, we concur with the conclusion of the Anglican – Lutheran European Regional Commission: 'There are no longer any serious obstacles on the way towards the establishment of full communion between our two Churches'. We 'acknowledge each other as true Churches of Christ preaching the same gospel, possessing a common apostolic ministry, and celebrating authentic sacraments' (*Helsinki Report,* 62-63).

72   Furthermore, in addition to the common sharing of fundamental beliefs and practices which we have listed, we wish to make the affirmations which follow:

73   We recognize that in each other's churches there exists a sustained and serious commitment to the apostolic mission of the Church.

74   We see ourselves already united by baptism in thankfulness to God for the gift of Jesus Christ, our Lord and Saviour, and for the sending of the Holy Spirit.

75 We acknowledge in each other's ministries of *episcope* the fruits of the presence of Jesus Christ and the activity of the Holy Spirit, in the offering of sacrifices of praise and thanksgiving, in the reflection of the faithful love of God towards the world, in care for the nurture and growth of all the faithful, and in commitment to the establishment of the kingdom of God in justice and peace for the whole earth.

76 We confess to God, to each other and to all Christian people how far, in our discharge of the ministry of *episcope,* our Churches have fallen short of the unity and continuity of the apostolic commission. We ask of each other forgiveness for our disregard of each other's gifts, for our lack of humility, and for our past toleration of our division.

77 We earnestly desire to remove those barriers which prevent the life of our churches from reflecting that unity of heart and mind which is God's gift to the people of God.

78 We commit ourselves to the obligation to take counsel together in reaching a common mind on how the mission of the people of God can most fruitfully be served in every place, so that there may be a united witness to the gospel, in word and deed, and a common enjoyment of the means of grace.

79 We intend thereby also to promote the unity of all churches with whom we are seeking, or have already discovered, the faith of the catholic Church.

80 We rejoice in rediscovering in each other our common inheritance of faith and of life, and in our unity in the One, Holy, Catholic, and Apostolic Church.

> Praise be to the God and Father of our Lord Jesus Christ, who has bestowed on us in Christ every spiritual blessing in the heavenly realms.

IV

Application to Anglicans and Lutherans

81 At our Consultation we addressed the question: 'In the light of our common mission, what needs to be re-formed in our respective expressions of *episcope*?' We also tried to visualize what patterns of leadership and oversight would be needed to meet the challenges of the next century. We were aware that all human institutions are subject to constant obsolescence and change. We cannot, therefore, commend uncritically either the re-appropriation of historic episcopate or the perpetuation of existing forms of the exercise of *episcope*.

82 Neither of our Churches is able to claim such a degree of faithfulness, that is, a continuity in either doctrine or order, as would enable it to sit in judgement on the other.

83 Nevertheless both our Churches have been given by God sufficient faithfulness to the apostolic gospel that today we can recognize each other as sister Churches.

84 The Churches of the Lutheran tradition have received as the focus for God's faithfulness to them the creeds of the early Church, the confessions of the sixteenth century, and the continuity of the ordained ministry through which the Word of God has been preached and the sacraments and rites of the Church have been administered.

85 The Churches of the Anglican Communion have received as the focus for God's faithfulness to them the

creeds of the early Church, the Book of Common Prayer
from the sixteenth century (revised periodically and adapted
regionally), and the continuity of the episcopal office
through which clergy have been ordained for the preaching
of the Word of God and the administration of the
sacraments and rites of the Church.

86 Formal recognition of each other's ministries so that
our Churches acknowledge a relationship of full communion between them cannot simply mean that neither Church
changes. Nor can it mean that either Church changes
merely to meet the expectations and requirements of the
other.

87 Rather Churches of both communions are being called
to acknowledge that the experience and practice of full
communion will involve them both and simultaneously in
changes and reforms.

88 Lutheran Churches are being asked to make four
changes in current practice, as follows:

89 All persons who exercise an ordained ministry of
episcope should receive the title of bishop or suffragan
bishop. (See Paragraph 57 and Appendix IV for historical
and other information on the titles currently in use in some
Lutheran churches.)

90 Because Lutherans understand the office of bishop as
pastoral (CA, XXVIII, 5 *et passim;* cf. *Lutheran Understanding of the Episcopal Office,* 1983, which states that 'episcopal
ministry and episcopal office denote the task of pastoral

leadership and spiritual supervision', pp. 3 ff.), constitutions should be revised so that bishops are elected to the same tenure of office as are congregational pastors, chaplains, and other pastoral ministers in the Church. That is, they should be elected and called until such time as death, retirement, or resignation terminate their incumbency. This may mean that Churches will also want to revise the procedures for identifying and nominating candidates for election to the ministry of bishop so that God's gifts of leadership and governance (1 Cor. 12.28) are properly recognized and called to office. Where appropriate, bishops and Churches should also establish and welcome structures for collegial and periodic review with the purpose of evaluating and improving the bishop's ministry.

91   In accordance with the canons of the Council of Nicaea the rites of installation for bishops should be revised so that there is a laying on of hands by at least three bishops. The involvement of three bishops in the installation of a bishop is the liturgical form by which the Church recognizes that the bishop serves the local or regional church through ties of collegiality which are links to the universal Church. Such participation of three bishops should express liturgically the fact that genuine consultation among bishops on the faith and life of the Church is expected in structure and practice. If we are in full communion with each other, one or more of the bishops at a Lutheran installation should be from a Church in the Anglican Communion. Lutherans can invite such participation by Anglican bishops for two reasons. First, in recognizing and acknowledging 'the full authenticity of the existing ministries of Lutheran churches' (see paragraph 94) Anglicans join Lutherans in affirming that

bishops have authority only through the gospel (CA XXVIII, 5-8) and thus serve the identity and unity of the Church given by the pure preaching of the gospel and the administration of the sacraments (CA VII, 2). Second, Lutherans have confessionally and historically recognized that the historic episcopate is a valuable symbol of unity and continuity in the Church (cf. LRCJC, *The Ministry in the Church,* 65, 66, and 80, together with the documentation in the footnotes). Such participation of Anglican bishops must be a symbol for mandatory mutual consultation and real interaction in *episcope.*

92 It should become the unfailing practice that only bishops or suffragan bishops should preside at all ordinations of clergy in their respective regions (synods, dioceses, churches, districts). This is consistent with much current practice in Lutheran Churches; and it is upheld in principle by the fact that Lutheran bishops or those who exercise *episcope* in Lutheran Churches must now authorize all ordinations at which they do not themselves preside.

93 Anglican Churches are being asked to make three changes in current practice, as follows:

94 Anglican Churches should make the necessary canonical revisions so that they can acknowledge and recognize the full authenticity of the existing ministries of Lutheran Churches. We believe that the basis for such action lies in the recognition that 'the apostolic succession in the episcopal office does not consist primarily in an unbroken chain of those ordaining to those ordained, but in a succession in the presiding ministry of a church, which

stands in the continuity of apostolic faith' (*The Ministry in the Church,* 62). Anglican Churches are here being asked for a major canonical revision in ordering their relationships to those Lutheran Churches which have bishops who are not in the historic episcopate and to those whose chief ministers exercising *episcope* are not called bishops. We believe that Anglicans are free to do this both by the grace and power of the Holy Spirit and because such action does not mean surrender of the gift of the historic episcopate. 'Full communion', the consequence of such acknowledgement and recognition, does not mean the organizational merger of Anglican and Lutheran Churches. Therefore Anglican Churches would continue to consecrate their own bishops and ordain their own clergy according to the ordinals now in use.

95   Anglican Churches and bishops should establish and welcome structures for collegial and periodic review with the purpose of evaluating and improving the bishop's ministry (see paragraph 90).

96   Anglican Churches should regularly invite Lutheran bishops to participate in the laying on of hands at the consecration and installation of Anglican bishops. Such participation must be a symbol for mandatory mutual consultation and real interaction in *episcope* (see paragraph 91).

97   We rejoice in the ways God's faithfulness has been manifested in our respective Churches. We receive and cultivate the faithfulness of God evident in the historic episcopate. We recognize and praise God for his faithfulness in preserving the apostolic mission and continuity of

the Church where the historic succession in the episcopate has been broken. We intend with these changes to enter into full communion, to create a single eucharistic community, to engage in fully shared mission, and thus to prepare for what structural implications may emerge. We trust that what we do will have significance for progress in other ecumenical relationships.

98   In all of this we wish to assure ourselves and our partners in ecumenical dialogue that these changes are not intended to imply and do not imply indifference to the gift and symbol of historic episcopate. We also assure our partners in bilateral and multilateral dialogue that we want to be mindful of our conversations with them and our commitments to them. No bilateral consensus or action can be blessed which ignores the Church in its many traditions and manifestations. What we do is always done in the sight of all (*in conspectu omnium*) and – in so far as we are granted insight – on behalf of all.

99   In addition to the above changes proposed for each of our Churches, we wish to pose questions which imply reform and renewal in the area of *episcope* to both of our Churches.

100   Are those exercising pastoral leadership and oversight in our Churches given the time and space to reflect on the priorities for mission in their regions, or have they become absorbed in and overloaded by administration? Is the administrative unit over which they preside frankly too big, so that their time and energy is all spent on the maintenance of a system rather than on the discernment of opportunity?

Does the scale of their responsibilities make them inattentive to the experience of those whose daily witness involves their standing on the edge of Church life? Has overfamiliarity with committee work, which indeed has its proper role, bred a lack of vision and of courage?

101   Are those in the episcopal office accessible enough to clergy and their families, not only in times of crisis but in an ongoing pastoral relationship? Do they take care not to foster an immature dependency, but rather encourage clergy to take responsibility for appraising their own ministry periodically, for reviewing their ministerial priorities, and for pursuing their own continuing education and spiritual refreshment? Do they also ensure that adequate resources are provided for offering personal help to clergy and their families in times of sickness, bereavement, domestic stress and financial difficulty?

102   Can those who exercise pastoral leadership and oversight escape the danger of being occupied too much with the affairs of the clergy, and also offer effective leadership in releasing and drawing together the talents of many individuals within the whole people of God? Can they set an example of leadership which is not autocratic but truly shared, facilitating collaborative styles of ministry and enabling the skills and insights of lay persons in every walk of life to be contributed to the Church's common life?

103   Has the Anglican or Lutheran view of what it means to be in apostolic succession whether of pedigree or pure confession become such a matter of pride that the mission of the Church has ceased to be a criterion by which the

Church is judged? Do those exercising *episcope*, whether Anglicans or Lutherans, consider they 'possess' the apostolic entitlement, or do they see themselves challenged and outstripped by its demands and responsibilities?

104   Is it really the case that those exercising *episcope* consult with each other? Have they substituted the goal of denominational coherence for the wider vision of the unity of all Christians? Have they become so absorbed in consultative or legislative problems and procedures within their own nation or province that they have ceased to care how their actions might influence other Christians in other parts of the world?

105   Has mutuality ceased between those exercising *episcope* in the Church and their own local communities? Have leaders ceased to understand the changing needs of congregations? Have they become so remote from the poor and those on the margins of society that they can no longer represent the ministry of one who was the friend of, and host to, sinners? Or conversely, do local congregations keep those who exercise *episcope* at bay, as though their ministry were thought to be an intrusion upon, or competitive with, the self-sufficient organization of a parish?

106   Do those exercising *episcope* in the Church expound and commend the Christian faith in a sustained way, not just preaching on special occasions or during isolated visits to congregations? Do they take real care to enlist the advice and help of those skilled in communications in the modern world, and to address those issues which are of urgent concern to people? Do they make the most of their corporate

teaching role as a conference of bishops, and provide collegial support to one another in the exercise of their teaching responsibilities?

107 Do those who exercise *episcope* understand their liturgical role to be central to their responsibilities, and do they carry it out in a creative way? Do they lead the offering of prayer and praise with a sense of awe and reverence, inspiring clergy and congregations to offer well prepared and heart-felt worship to God? Do they maintain a proper balance between word and sacrament in their programme of public worship events? Do they encourage the renewal of liturgy, and hold together diverse styles of worship within the Church's life? Do they take care to retain those skills which they now exercise less often than they did at an earlier phase of their ministries? Do they perform their liturgical tasks in a manner which symbolizes that all ministry is shared with others?

108 Do those exercising *episcope* show in their own personal lives Christ-like qualities? Do they give an example of holiness, love, humility and simplicity of life? Are they generous and hospitable? Is their style of life influenced too much by the patterns of leadership that are dominant in the culture where they live? Is it evident that they are dedicated to unselfish service, and are open to be touched by the sufferings of others? Do they give the time and space needed for prayer, study, rest, recreation and family life, and avoid being devoured by unreasonable public expectations of their office?

109 Are those chosen for leadership given the ceremonial trappings of prominence, but denied the ability to exercise

their responsibilities? Is *effective* leadership vested in reality in persons who, by reason of their obscurity in a bureaucracy, are not accountable to the whole Church? Are the realities of the exercise of power effectively disguised from view, and is it silently presumed that power can only be exercised competitively and never co-operatively? Are Churches so frightened by the danger of authoritarianism that their systems of checks and balances destroy any capacity to respond in moments of special challenge and danger?

110 These are but some of the enquiries which follow from the argument we have advanced. They are based in the account we have given of the requirements for the mission of the Church, on the understanding that the apostolic ministry must be a ministry engaged in, and facilitating the mission of the whole Church. *Episcope* is a ministry of service, exercised with the co-operation of the whole community. Leaders are to 'manifest and exercise the authority of Christ in the way Christ himself revealed God's authority to the world, by committing their life to the community' (BEM, M 16). When we ask whether leaders in communities other than our own do this with faithfulness, we are engaged in a process which inevitably involves self-examination. Our conclusion is that both our communions are called in the first place to penitence.

V

Practical Steps

111   Here we consider by what practical steps Anglicans and Lutherans can realize Full Communion.

112   *Step 1:*   Each Regional or National Church's governing body:

(a) affirms the agreement in faith as expressed in certain specified documents (eg. paragraphs 61-70 of this Report).

(b) recognizes the Church of .... as a true Church of the Gospel etc (see BEM, M 53, [a] or [b]).

113   *Step 2:*   Create provisional structures to express the degree of unity so far achieved and to promote further growth. These could include the following examples, though the time scale could vary region by region:

(a) Eucharistic Sharing and Joint Common Celebration of the Eucharist;

(b) meetings of Church leaders for regular prayer, reflection and consultation, thus beginning joint *episcope;*

(c) mutual invitation of Church leaders, clergy and laity, to synods, with a right to speak;

(d) common agencies wherever possible;

(e) explore the possibility of adjusting boundaries to assist local and regional co-operation;

(f) Covenants among Church leaders to collaborate in *episcope;*

(g) joint pastoral appointments for special projects;

(h) joint theological education and training courses;

(i) sharing of information and documents;

(j) joint mission programmes;

(k) agreed syllabuses for Christian education in schools, joint materials for catechesis and adult study;

(l) co-operation over liturgical forms, cycles of inter-cession, lectionaries and homiletic materials;

(m) welcoming isolated clergy or diaspora congregations into the life of a larger group (see ALERC *Helsinki Report,* 5);

(n) interchange of ministers to the extent permitted by canon law;

(o) twinning (partnership) between congregations and communities;

(p) joint programmes of diaconal ministry and reflection on issues of social responsibility;

(q) joint retreats and devotional materials.

The ACC and LWF should be asked to give their full sup-port to Churches making such provisional arrangements.

114 *Step 3:* The actions taken in Steps 1 and 2 form the basis and motivation for the implementation of the recom-mendations in paragraphs 88-96.

115 *Step 4:* Together representatives (including lay members, ordained ministers and Church leaders) of both Churches publicly celebrate the establishment of full com-munion. This liturgical occasion should include the follow-ing elements:

(a) penitence for past shortcomings;

(b) declaration of joint faith;

(c) reaffirmation of baptismal vows;

(d) mutual greeting by sharing the Peace by the right hand of fellowship, so as to avoid any suggestion of reordination, mutual recommissioning of ministries, crypto-validation, or any other ambiguity;

(e) a celebration of the Eucharist;

(f) covenant to work together and become closely involved in one another's corporate life, with the long-term aim of fuller unity;

(g) a personal covenant of the Church leaders to collaborate in *episcope*. (It is intended that new leaders should enter the same covenant on assuming office.)

116 *Notes:* We understand these steps to be compatible with those proposed by LRCJC, *Facing Unity,* pp. 58 ff.

This process should be constantly open to further ecumenical initiatives with other Churches, and is not intended to be exclusive (see above paragraph 97).

After Step 4 joint consecration and installation of bishops and ordination of new ministers should be possible.

APPENDIX I

Anglican – Lutheran Consultation on Episcope

Anglican Participants

The Revd Canon Keith
  Chittleborough
The Revd Dr L. William
  Countryman
The Revd Dr Alyson Barnett
  Cowan
The Revd Dr Kortright Davis
Dr David Ford
The Ven. Nehemiah Shihala
  Hamupembe
The Rt Revd Russell Hatton
Ms Nangula Hauwanga
The Revd Dr Richard A.
  Norris Jr.
Professor Patricia Page

Lutheran Participants

The Revd Sven Eric Brodd
Dr Faith Burgess
The Rt Revd Herbert W.
  Chilstrom
The Revd Dr Donald Juel
The Revd Nathan E Kapofi
The Revd Dr Robert
  Marshall
The Revd Julius Paul
Ms Annette Smith
Dr Nelvin Vos

Orthodox Consultant

The Revd Professor Basil
  Zion

Roman Catholic Consultant

The Revd William Marravee

The members of the Continuation Committee (Appendix II)
were also present.

APPENDIX II

Anglican – Lutheran International Continuation Committee

Anglican Participants

The Rt Revd David Tustin (Co-Chair)

The Revd Professor J. M. Flynn

The Rt Revd Charles Mwaigoga

The Rt Revd John G. Savarimuthu

The Revd Professor Stephen W. Sykes

Lutheran Participants

The Rt Revd Sebastian Kolowa (Co-Chair)

The Revd Dr Walter Bouman

The Rt Revd Tore Furberg

The Revd Christa Grengel

The Revd Dr B. C. Paul

The Revd Dr Karheinz Schmale*

Consultants

The Revd. Dr William A. Norgren*

The Revd Dr Jan Womer

Staff

The Revd George Braund

Ms Vanessa Wilde

The Revd Dr Eugene L. Brand

Mrs Irmhild Reichen-Young

*Not present at the Niagara Meeting.

Professor Marianne H. Micks retired from the Continuation Committee for health reasons immediately before the Niagara Meeting.

APPENDIX III

Anglican – Lutheran International Continuation Committee

The Marie Reparatrice Centre, Wimbledon, England
13th – 17th October 1986

REPORT

Background

1 The Anglican – Lutheran International Continuation Committee (ALICC) was appointed by the Anglican Consultative Council (ACC) and the Lutheran World Federation (LWF) on the recommendation (IIb.) of the Anglican – Lutheran Joint Working Group, which met at Cold Ash, England, 28th November – 3rd December 1983. The meeting produced a report entitled 'Anglican – Lutheran Relations, Report of the Anglican – Lutheran Joint Working Group' (*The Cold Ash Report*), which provides essential background to the whole progress of Anglican – Lutheran relations in recent times. In it the Group stated that 'the last 15 years have seen remarkable convergence between the Anglican and Lutheran Communions and their member churches' and recommended their respective bodies to 'move with urgency towards the fullest possible ecclesial recognition and the goal of full communion' (p. 16). The Group had before it:

Anglican – Lutheran International Conversations, 1970-2. *The Pullach Report.*

Lutheran – Episcopal Dialogue I, 1972, and Lutheran – Episcopal Dialogue II, 1981 (LED II).

Anglican – Lutheran Dialogue, 1983. *The Helsinki Report* of the Anglican – Lutheran European Regional Commission.

The Agreement adopted by the Conventions of The American Lutheran Church, the Association of Evangelical Lutheran Churches, the Episcopal Church in the USA and the Lutheran Church in America, September 1982.

2   The Task of the Continuation Committee is first to co-ordinate information about developments in Anglican – Lutheran relations in various parts of the world, and then, on the basis of an assessment of the total picture, to foster and to stimulate new initiatives. It reports to its parent bodies.

3   Recent Developments

ALICC received the following reports:

The Final Report of the Australian Anglican – Lutheran Conversations, 1972-1984.

A Report by the Board for Mission and Unity of the Church of England on Anglican – Lutheran and other international dialogues (GS 685), June 1985.

The Report and Recommendations of the Canadian Anglican – Lutheran Dialogue, April 1986.

A Report from the 8th Theological Conversations between the Evangelische Kirche in Deutschland (EKD) and the Church of England, April 1986.

It also received William A. Norgren's Study Guide to Lutheran – Episcopal Relations, *What Can We Share?* (1985); reports on the questionnaires regarding Anglican – Lutheran Relations throughout the world, prepared by the ACC and the LWF; and the report of the Archbishop of Canterbury's visit to and address at the Lutheran Church in America Convention, Milwaukee, in August 1986; *Changing Anglican – Lutheran Relations,* William A. Norgren 1985; *Towards Full Communion,* William G. Rusch. 1985; *Facing Unity.* Models, Forms and

Phases of Catholic – Lutheran Church Fellowship. Roman Catholic – Lutheran Joint Commission. Published by the Lutheran World Federation, 1985.

4   These documents by no means constitute a comprehensive coverage of all developments, and the Committee acknowledges the difficulty in assembling all the relevant information, as the different member churches respond to international or national bilateral reports and other documents. It is also the case that from some smaller Lutheran and Anglican churches we have little or no information about ecumenical developments.

5   Oral reports were delivered by the members present at the ALICC of developments in a number of major theatres of Anglican – Lutheran interaction, including Tanzania, Malaysia, India (relations between Lutherans and the Church of South India), North America and Europe.

6   *Assessment*

It is clear from all the information before us that further highly significant steps are being taken on a regional basis to promote ever-increasing closeness of relationship, despite the lack of an international dialogue. We wish to draw attention to certain examples of this co-operation:

(a) *Tanzania:* The Tanzanian Christian Council enables heads of all non-Roman Catholic churches to meet for two or three days every year to discuss things of mutual concern. Out of these annual contacts church leaders in Tanzania are very often great friends. On the basis of this friendship some Anglican bishops have received invitations to the consecration of Lutheran bishops and the same has been true of some Anglican consecrations.

(b) *USA:* In its third series, the Lutheran – Episcopal Dialogue in the USA (LED III) has nearly completed work on a document mandated by the churches: 'The Gospel and its Implications'. This is an attempt to make use of the eschatological perspective proving fruitful in current biblical and theological studies as the churches seek to be more faithful in engaging in mission in terms of ecumenism, evangelization and ethics. The dialogue has agreed to recommend to the respective churches some form of recognizing each other's central documents, that Lutherans recognize the Book of Common Prayer and Episcopalians recognize the Augsburg Confession and Luther's Small Catechism. There are increasing instances of regular consultation between Episcopal and Lutheran bishops, of shared ministry by and in parishes, of regular study conferences of clergy from both churches and large gatherings for dialogue and worship. Virtually every part of the USA has had some formal joint celebrations of the Eucharist by Lutheran and Episcopal bishops.

(c) *Canada:* After a process beginning in October 1983, the Canadian Anglican – Lutheran Dialogue has submitted a report to the churches containing brief agreed statements on Justification, the Eucharist, Apostolicity, and Ordained Ministry. The report proposes that the churches acknowledge each other 'as churches where the Gospel is truly preached and taught'. The report requests the churches to initiate internally a period of study (1986-1989) of the agreed statements and to declare a relationship of interim sharing of eucharist beginning in 1989 with an evaluation of this experience to be made in 1995. A number of other actions are also encouraged.

(d) *Europe:* Study and preparatory work has been commissioned by the Church of England, the Evangelische Kirche in Deutschland and the Bund der Evangelischen Kirchen in der DDR for closer ecumenical relationships between these churches. A consultation of these churches is to be held in February 1987.

Pastoral and theological consultations and exchanges have been taking place every two years between the Church of England and the Scandinavian churches, drawing upon a long history of official Church of England relationships with the Churches of Sweden and Finland.

(e) *Australia:* Though the Australian Lutheran Churches are not part of the LWF, we noted that a fruitful dialogue with Anglicans has been conducted since 1974, involving strands of Lutheranism not normally engaged in common ecumenical endeavour and covering a wide range of topics.

(f) *India:* The Anglican dioceses became part of the Church of South India and the Church of North India. In 1947 the Lutheran churches in South India (about a million Christians) entered into union negotiations with the Church of South India, and they found a remarkable agreement in essential theological issues, but for reasons, largely non-theological, could not form one body. Nevertheless there are close relations between them in various aspects of life, especially in joint theological seminaries. Now the Lutheran churches in South India have become part of the United Evangelical Lutheran Churches in India.

7   It is apparent that the process of convergence described in *The Cold Ash Report* is continuing. The theological agreements reached in international and regional dialogues have facilitated shared life, and, as so often happens, Christian living and theological reflection have mutually supported and enriched each other.

The Present Situation

8   In some contexts, it appears that shared life is a consequence of theological agreement and the process of reception. After the agreement reached in international and regional dialogues it

becomes possible for developments to occur in particular places, where responsible Christian judgement demands a new initiative. For instance, an Anglican bishop finds himself asking a Lutheran bishop to exercise oversight of churches in an emergency.

9   These developments are of different kinds, reminding us of the multi-faceted nature of the process of reconciliation. In some contexts, for good historical reasons, great emphasis has to be placed on theological discussion and the building of consensus; in other places what is crucial is making a reality of the sharing of oversight and mutual consultation; in other places, again, what is vital is breaking down cultural or communal barriers in the life of the whole church. It is our experience that the establishment of priorities in each situation has to be determined by the imperatives of the Church's mission. Mission and ecumenism are inseparable, and have to be worked out region to region. Not all developments are capable of being applied universally. Some rest on understandings and judgements which are, as yet, incapable of verbal formulation, but which have resulted from responsible judgements in the face of particular needs or opportunities.

10   It is also true that there are places where the two churches live side by side and there are no signs of joint theological activity.

Future Work

11   We have begun, and must continue, to identify the resources which we are discovering in one another. We have already received much from each other in our traditions of worship and liturgy, music and hymnody, historical and theological study, stewardship and spirituality. We continue to receive gifts through the lessons learned by sister churches in times of hard-

ship and persecution, through the various ways our churches have sought to relate to social and political contexts with equally various degrees of faithfulness. It is a part of the task of this committee to discover and identify as many resources as God has given us, to evaluate their role in our common life and growing relationships, and to urge and facilitate the wider sharing of these resources between our communions. That these resources cannot always or easily be translated from one context to another must be remembered. The historical ambiguities present in our strengths and gifts dare not be ignored. But gifts remain gifts, even in brokenness and ambiguity, and they can be means used by God to further the great gifts of reconciliation and unity.

12 *Rethinking our goals.* Since the Cold Ash meeting, questions have surfaced about the way 'full communion' is described and defined in the Cold Ash Report and its relationship with the anticipated goal of other actual or potential forms or models of church unity. Because of these and other questions we recognize that one of our tasks must be the rethinking and reformulating of the meaning of 'full communion'. We are persuaded that such reformulation can take place only in the context of our growing common experience with one another.

13 *Consultation on Episcope.* Another of our tasks must be to discuss the relationship between Apostolic Succession, the Ministry of the whole people of God, Episcopacy and the historic episcopate. We propose to do this in a consultation which would see ministry in relation to the mission of the Church today. This Consultation will be held in 1987 and our proposal for it is as follows:

Theme: *Episcope* in Relation to the Mission of the Church Today.

Questions to be addressed in the context of Anglican – Lutheran relations:

61

(a) How was *episcope* exercised in the New Testament and the Early Church? How did it relate to Mission?

This question demands that attention be paid to the sociological as well as theological factors underlying historical developments as the Church moved toward more structured community life for the sake of mission, at varying rates of speed in different areas. It presupposes that there was no uniformity of development, all developments have equal or enduring validity.

(b) What is the mission of the Church in the 21st century? What is the Church's prophetic role?

Both parts of this question demand answers set in a variety of cultural and geographical contexts. It cannot be fruitfully addressed in only abstract terms of global import.

(c) How is *episcope* related to the ministry of the whole people of God?

Implicit in this question is the fact that the whole people of God exercises *episcope* in a variety of 'styles' appropriate (or inappropriate!) to our different cultural contexts. It may be that some styles of leadership are more suitable in Christian communities than others. The Consultation should keep the relation between leadership and service in mind.

(d) In light of our common mission, what needs to be reformed in our respective expressions of *episcope*?

Discussion of this key question is central to the task of the Consultation. Clearly it needs to take into account insights gleaned from the previous questions and answers. It asks, in effect, how can we do our job better?

(e) What can we do together in *episcope*? How can we initiate and enable the joint exercise of *episcope* as a gradual process?

(i) What light is thrown on this by our churches' responses

to the Ministry section of the BEM document – especially paragraphs 23-25?

(ii) What light is thrown on this by our respective bilateral dialogues with the Roman Catholic Church?

Again, this question presupposes a number of different answers for our different contexts. It follows that no single process can emerge, following a single time-table. Recognizing this, the question invites creative 'dreaming'.

(f) How do we formulate attainable goals for our common mission?

The emphasis in this question is on attainable goals. What criteria are appropriate for judging whether a goal is attainable? That ours is a common mission is a presupposition, presumably needing no further elucidation.

14 *Further Steps.* There are further concrete steps which we can take and/or propose to the churches on the way toward realization of the goal of full communion between our churches. We have identified the following tasks:

(a) We should identify areas in which our churches need to be better informed about each other, where misleading or outdated perceptions inhibit trust and co-operation, understanding and commitment to unity. This is especially the case where geographical separation prevents continued living experience of one another, where common challenges and resources are not evident to one another, where stereotypes and caricatures prejudice our relationships and weaken our movement towards full communion.

(b) We need to develop forms and forums for common attention to the Scriptures, that is, letting ourselves be corporately challenged by what the Scriptures have to say to us today. Increased joint work on lectionaries, homiletical studies, catechetical and adult study materials could be undertaken.

(c) In so far as possible, members, clergy and leaders of our churches need encouragement to share in common worship, beginning with the Eucharist hospitality which is now quite generally possible between Anglicans and Lutherans. We also need to cultivate mutual prayer and intercession for one another in concrete and specific ways. We need joint attention to the cultivation of discipleship grounded in our common and mutually recognized Baptism.

(d) One important and newly recognized way to understand the Lutheran reformation confession of 'justification by faith' is that it is not so much a new or additional doctrine, but rather it is an instruction to pastors about how they are to preach and teach the Christ of the ancient classic doctrines so that Christ is encountered as promise, not threat, and so that Christ is therefore received by faith, not by some inappropriate response (eg. 'works'). This creates an opportunity for renewed and common theological and catechetical attention to the Apostles' and Nicene creeds, that is, to the classical Christological and Trinitarian dogmas, so that they are experienced as Gospel confession rather than as ecclesiastical ideology. This is a common study task in which our traditions both need and can assist each other.

(e) Even though our churches do not agree fully on the meaning or expression of episcopacy, we can give attention to the development and cultivation of forms for consultation of leaders with each other. Simultaneously, the leadership needs to encourage the interaction of clergy, congregations, seminarians, and theologicans for purposes of shared experience in worship, study and mission.

(f) We need to look at the authentic apostolic continuity which both our churches evidence, although not always in identical forms, and which links us both to the church of all ages. Simultaneously we need to increase our awareness of the diversity of contexts throughout the world in which our churches live and function, often side-by-side.

(g) We intend to ask how the practice of interim sharing of the Eucharist, begun in the USA, could be effected in other contexts.

(h) We intend to describe and propose theological and pastoral exchanges in regions where these are not already taking place as a way of implementing the concrete steps identified above because shared life is reciprocally related to theological agreement.

15 *Our Witness.* All these tasks are to be understood in terms of the Church's witness and evangelism, which includes worship and prayer, diaconic service, and attention to issues of peace with justice.

16 *Lay Leadership.* We regard as fundamental to the relationship of our churches that the laity exercise responsibility for leadership in ecumenical mission and that our envisioning of concrete steps into the future make provision for such exercise of lay responsibility.

APPENDIX IV

Ordained Ministry in German Lutheran Churches

Present structures date from World War I when the change in governmental structures put an end to church structures based on provincial rulers (Landesherrliche Kirchenregiment). A new solution emerged: Das synodale Bischofsamt. The concept of shared leadership between bishop and synod has become widespread among Lutherans. Even in the Nordic countries where the office of bishop retained a more 'traditional' structure, synods have been introduced which share the leadership responsibility for the church.

1. BISCHOF (Landesbischof)

Shares authority with synod which elects and can remove from office. Primary duties: visitation and ordination. Specific duties: responsibility for biblically sound doctrine, proclamation and counsel, congregations, pastors and other church workers, care for the training of church workers, advising theological faculties and church training centres, issuing pastoral letters, representing the church in the public sector, promoting ecumenical relationships.

2. LEITENDER BISCHOF

Chairs Bishops' Conference of VELKD/VELK and its Church Council. Elected for a term by the General Synod of VELKD/VELK.

Because of the magnitude of most of the provincial churches (Landeskirchen), *episcope* is exercised within geographical subdivisions by 'assistant/suffragan bishops' with the various titles listed below. In some provincial churches there are two levels of subdivision – e.g. the provincial church of Bavaria has districts (Kirchenkreise) which are subdivided into deaneries (Dekanatsbezirke); the provincial church of Hanover has dioceses

(Sprengel) which are subdivided into districts (Kirchenkreise). In practice the chief tasks of the 'assistant/suffragan bishops' are visitation and ordination.

3. SUPERINTENDENT (Landessuperintendent), e.g. Hanover.

4. DEKAN (Kreisdekan), e.g. Bavaria.

5. PROPST, e.g. Brunswick.

6. PRÄLAT, e.g. Württemburg.

7. OBERKIRCHENRAT, e.g. Thuringia (OKR most often designates a top-level administrative officer whether ordained or not. In Thuringia, however, some OKR are 'assistant/suffragan bishops' with several superintendents under them.)

It is scope of service and assigned duties which distinguish bishops from pastors; the relationship is not hierarchical. The unity of the one ministry of word and sacrament is emphasized.

8. PASTOR/PFARRER
Minister of word and sacrament in the congregation.

9. VIKAR
Person engaged in supervised parish work prior to ordination (internship).

Cf. Tröger, G., 'Das synodale Bischofsamt', TRE VI (1980), pp. 694-697.

Eugene L. Brand

APPENDIX V

Bibliography

Anglican – Lutheran International Conversations, 1970-72. *The Pullach Report.* SPCK, London, 1973.

Anglican – Lutheran Dialogue, The Report of the European Commission, 1982. *The Helsinki Report.* SPCK, London, 1983.

Anglican – Lutheran Relations, Report of the Anglican – Lutheran Joint Working Group, 1983. *The Cold Ash Report.* ACC, London / LWF, Geneva, 1983.

Anglican – Roman Catholic International Commission, The Final Report. CTS / SPCK, London, 1982.

Baptism, Eucharist and Ministry, Faith and Order Paper No. 111. WCC, Geneva, 1982.

Growth in Agreement, ed. Meyer and Vischer. Paulist Press, New York / WCC, Geneva, 1984.

Lutherans and Catholics in Dialogue IV, *Eucharist and Ministry.* US Catholic Conference, Washington / LWF, New York, 1970.

Lutheran – Episcopal Dialogue, The Report of the Lutheran – Episcopal Dialogue, Second Series, 1976-1980. Forward Movement, Cincinnati, 1981.

Lutheran – Roman Catholic Joint Commission, *The Ministry in the Church.* LWF, Geneva, 1982.

Lutheran – Roman Catholic Joint Commission, *Facing Unity.* Models, Forms and Phases of Catholic – Lutheran Church Fellowship. LWF, Geneva, 1985.

Lutheran Understanding of the Episcopal Office. LWF, Geneva, 1985.

Unity of the Churches, H. Fries and K. Rahner. Philadelphia, 1985.

What Can We Share? A Lutheran Episcopal Resource and Study Guide. Compiled by William A. Norgren. Forward Movement, Cincinnati, 1985.

APPENDIX VI

Papers Presented at the Consultation

Donald Juel: Episcope in the New Testament.

Stephen W. Sykes: Response to 'Episcope in the New Testament'.

Richard A. Norris Jr: The Bishop in the Church of Late Antiquity.

Walter R. Bouman: The concept of Episcope in the Lutheran bilateral dialogues.

Robert J. Marshall: Episcope and the mission of the Church in the 21st Century.

Kortright Davis: Can the Church be saved?

John G. Savarimuthu: The prophetic role of Episcope in a Muslim country with special reference to Malaysia.

Sebastian Kolowa: Efforts towards church union in East Africa (Tanzania).

Keith S. Chittleborough: How is Episcope related to the ministry of the whole people of God?

Nelvin Vos: To be the Body of Christ in the World.

Faith Burgess: Episcope and the laity.

G. Russell Hatton: How is Episcope related to the ministry of the whole people of God?

Sven-Erik Brodd: Episcopacy as the fundamental and communal ministry in the Church: Some preliminary remarks.

L. William Countryman: Mission and the Reform of Episcope.

David F. Ford: In the light of our common mission, what needs to be reformed in our respective expressions of Episcope?

Patricia N. Page: In the light of our common mission, what needs to be reformed in our Anglican expression of Episcope?

Jan L. Womer: In the light of our common mission, what needs to be reformed in our respective expressions of Episcope?

Copies of these papers can be obtained from LWF, P.O. Box 66, 1211 Geneva 20, Switzerland.